Buddy, My Best Friend, Moves to a Place Called Heaven

My Story About My Dog

Written and Created by

Joe "The Gamer" Petraro

Pictures by Joe Petraro and Anne Petraro

Fulton Books, Inc.
Meadville, PA

Published by Fulton Books 2021

ISBN 978-1-63710-284-8 (paperback)
ISBN 978-1-63710-286-2 (hardcover)
ISBN 978-1-63710-285-5 (digital)

Printed in the United States of America

DEDICATION

For Councilman Anthony D'Esposito who
always makes me strive to do better

Joe woke up sad. Just yesterday, like every single day of his life, Buddy kissed him good morning. They had the best ever morning routine. He laid in bed, imagining Buddy was still home.

Buddy licked his face, and Joe would give him kisses back. When Buddy went outside to go to the bathroom, Mom always got frustrated. Joe would go to the bathroom *outside*! *With Buddy*! Even Penny, Joe's other dog, would shake her head at them in disbelief.

Buddy did everything Joe did. He went with him to train for karate, spent time with him playing video games, and they slept together every night. When Joe took his bath, Buddy sat at the bathroom floor, waiting. They ate together. The best was when Joe snuck food to eat with Bud! Midnight snacks!

As Joe laid in bed, thinking about Buddy, Penny came to check on Joe. Joe started to cry. It was snotty, and the worst cry he ever cried. Nothing Penny could do was helping. Penny was sad too and whimpered with Joe. After all, her brother Buddy just moved to heaven the night before.

8

Mom, Dad, Joe, and Penny sat together and cried. The night before felt like a dream. Buddy went peacefully to heaven after cuddling all day with the family in his favorite spot on the bed. Joe asked lots of questions about heaven. He knew his grandparents were there but was worried if Buddy was okay.

Mom told Joe crying was healthy. Joe and the family shared their emotions and talked about memories of their beloved dog. Buddy was free of pain and didn't need any medicine in heaven. They talked about all the happy times. As they took the time to be together and talk, something happened.

One by one, things were delivered to the house. Friends sent flowers, food, books, balloons, and all sorts of love for Buddy. You see, Buddy moved to heaven the day before his thirteenth birthday. Even though Joe was so sad, he felt so happy to celebrate Buddy's move to heaven *and* his birthday. The love and gifts helped the family so much.

One of the things Joe received was a book from his favorite librarian, Heather, called *Dog Heaven*. Once Joe read this, he understood all about life! Buddy didn't die… He just moved to heaven! Buddy had such an important life. He helped so many people. You see, Buddy was a therapy dog, a friend, a brother, a son, a neighbor, and so much more. He had been through a lot as he got older and kept fighting to stay alive for his family. Buddy was tired now. He wished his family understood, and he communicated that with them that last day they had together. Buddy was ready to move. He didn't need a suitcase. In heaven, everything you will ever need is there!

Even though Joe was going to miss his dog, probably forever and ever, he knew just how great Buddy's new home was! He can even sleep in a cloud and secretly visit Joe every day! Mom and Dad even told Joe he's with all his other animal and people friends who moved to heaven already.

You see, when our body gets tired, our soul's energy moves to heaven. It's kind of like moving to a new home. People who still live in the old home feel sad, but it's actually…like being born!

Buddy still loves Joe. Joe still feels him all around him. People who moved to heaven are kind of like superheroes! They have the best lives and wish their families at their old homes knew all about it.

Joe understood now and wrote this book so everyone can be excited about just how cool moving to heaven is!

Run free, Buddy!

Joe loves you forever!

ABOUT THE AUTHOR

 Joseph Petraro is from New York, where he resides with his parents and dog, Penny. He attends St. Raymond School and is a second grader. Joseph became a published author at age six, and this is his second book. When he lost his dog, Buddy, he decided to process his grief by writing a story about grief and loss that would help others. While Joseph isn't writing stories or drawing, he loves spending time making his YouTube videos (@joethegamer), training for karate, being a Cub Scout, and making others laugh. Joseph loves to give back to others. All proceeds he's made, he donates to charity.

CPSIA information can be obtained
at www.ICGtesting.com
Printed in the USA
BVHW052022170521
607556BV00010B/1517

9 781637 102848